Solar System

KINGFISHER

a Houghton Mifflin Company imprint
222 Berkeley Street
Boston, Massachusetts 02116
www.houghtonmifflinbooks.com

First published in 2004
2 4 6 8 10 9 7 5 3 1

1TR/0504/PROSP/RNB(RNB)/140MA

LIBRARY OF CONGRESS CATALOGING-IN-PUBLICATION DATA
Goldsmith, Mike, Dr.
Solar system/Mike Goldsmith.—1st ed.
p. cm.—(Kingfisher young knowledge)
Includes index.
1. Solar system—Juvenile literature. [1. Solar system.] I.Title. II.
Series.
QB501.3.G63 2004
523.2—dc22
2003026849

ISBN 0-7534-5773-3

Editor: Jennifer Schofield
Coordinating editor: Caitlin Doyle
Designer: Joanne Brown
Cover designer: Mike Buckley
Picture manager: Cee Weston-Baker
Picture researcher: Harriet Merry
Artwork archivists: Wendy Allison and Jennifer Lord
DTP manager: Nicky Studdart
DTP operator: Primrose Burton
Production controller: Oonagh Phelan
Indexer: Sheila Clewley

Printed in China

Acknowledgments
The Publisher would like to thank the following for permission to reproduce their material. Every care has been
taken to trace copyright holders. However, if there have been unintentional omissions or failure to trace
copyright holders, we apologize and will, if informed, endeavor to make corrections in any future edition.
b = bottom, *c* = center, *l* = left, *t* = top, *r* = right

Cover: Cassini probe: Science Photo Library (SPL); Earth's surface: SPL; 2–3 National Geographic; 4–5 NASA/Corbis;
6–7 NASA/SPL; 8*bl* Getty Images; 8–9 Getty Images; 10*cl* SPL; 10–11 NASA; 11*b* Corbis; 12–13 NASA/Corbis; 13*tl* Corbis;
13*bl* Mary Evans Picture Library; 16 Getty Images; 17*t* Getty Images; 18–19 Corbis; 18*r* NASA; 19*t* Getty Images;
19*b* Getty Images; 20–21 NASA; 21*tr* NASA; 21*bl* NASA; 22*bl* Galaxy; 22*cr* NASA/SPL; 23*t* Corbis; 23*b* NASA; 24*c* SPL;
24–25 NASA; 25*b* Kobal Collection; 26–27*t* NASA/SPL; 27*cl* NASA/SPL; 27*br* Corbis; 28–29 Corbis; 30*c* SPL; 30–31 Corbis;
31*tr* Corbis; 32–33 NASA/SPL; 33*tr* NASA/SPL; 37*br* NASA/SPL; 38*bl* The Art Archive; 38–39 Corbis; 39*br* Corbis;
40–41*t* Getty Images; 40–41*b* Galaxy Picture Library; 42–43 NASA/Corbis; 47*br* Alamy Images; 48*br* Corbis.

Commissioned artwork on pages 34–35 and 40–44 by Daniel Shutt; commissioned photography on pages 44–47 by Andy Crawford
Project maker and photo shoot coordinator: Miranda Kennedy
Thank you to models Holly Hadaway and Sonnie Nash.

KFYK Kingfisher Young Knowledge

Solar System

Dr. Mike Goldsmith

KINGFISHER
BOSTON

Contents

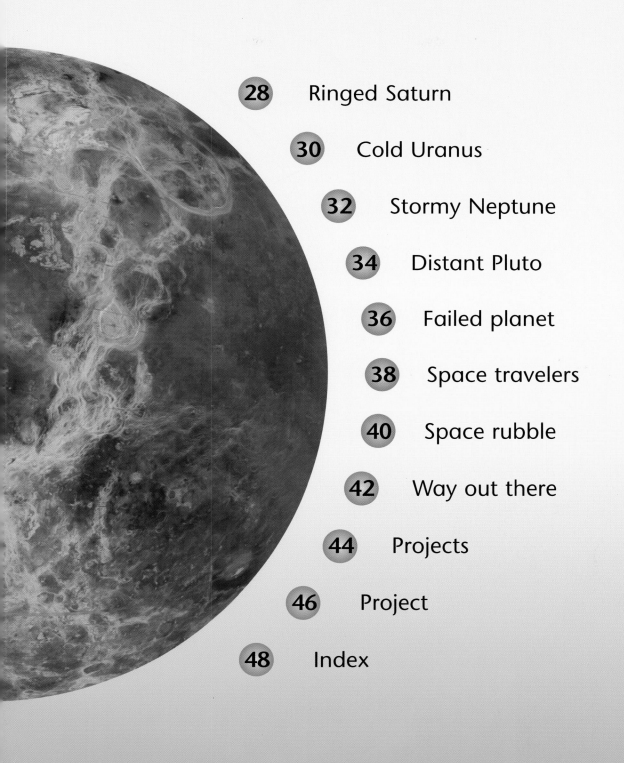

Solar system

The Earth that we live on, the Sun, and the Moon are all parts of the solar system. It is called the solar system because everything moves around the Sun, and solar means "of the Sun."

Other worlds

There are nine planets in the solar system, and Earth is just one of them. Most of the planets also have moons moving around them.

Sun

Mars

Earth

Venus

Mercury

Uranus

Pluto

Neptune

Saturn

Jupiter

Space rocks

The Sun, planets, and moons are not the only things in the solar system. There are comets, asteroids, meteoroids, dust, and gases too. Comets are like huge dirty snowballs. Asteroids are giant chunks of rock, and meteoroids are small pieces of rock.

Around and around

All nine planets in the solar system travel through space, going around the Sun. The time that it takes a planet to move around the Sun once is called a year.

The pull of gravity

The force that pulls things toward each other is called gravity. If you throw a soccer ball into the air, it is gravity that pulls it down again. The Sun's gravity holds the planets in place. If there was no gravity, Earth would fall into pieces, and you would be thrown into space.

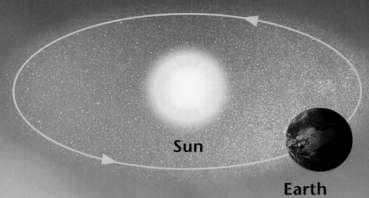

Sun

Earth

Around the Sun

It takes around 365 days for Earth to orbit the Sun. Planets closer to the Sun have shorter orbits, so they move around it quicker. Mercury's year lasts 88 days.

Day and night

Each planet also spins around itself, causing it to have day and night. On other planets these are not the same length of time as Earth's. The days on Venus are 243 times longer than ours!

orbit—*the path of one object around another object in space*

Fiery star

The Sun is the only star in the solar system. It is so big that one million Earths could fit inside it! The Sun is also very hot—much hotter than an oven.

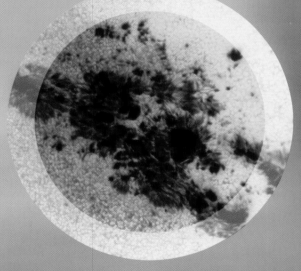

Spotty Sun
The surface of the Sun is always moving. Sometimes dark, cool spots form on the Sun's surface. These spots are called sunspots.

star—an enormous glowing ball of very hot gas

Great balls of fire

Prominences are giant masses of gas thrown off by the Sun. They look just like the leaping flames of a fire.

Warning! Hot Sun

It is dangerous to look directly at the Sun. When you play in the sunshine, always wear a hat, sunglasses, and sunscreen.

dangerous—*not safe*

Fast Mercury

Mercury is a small planet that orbits very close to the Sun. The Sun's light makes Mercury's days very hot, but nights on Mercury are bitterly cold—much colder than any freezer. This is because there is no air to stop the heat from escaping.

Rocks galore!

The surface of Mercury is dry and rocky with gigantic cliffs. Mercury also has huge craters (hollows) that were caused by falling rocks millions of years ago.

Mighty *Mariner*

The spacecraft *Mariner 10* flew past Mercury three times in 1974 and 1975. It took photographs of around one half of the planet.

God of speed

According to the myths of ancient Rome, Mercury was the messenger of the gods. He was supposed to fly quickly because he had wings on his heels.

Roasting Venus

Venus is the closest planet to Earth. On Venus the sky is yellow and cloudy. The clouds trap the Sun's heat, which makes Venus an extremely hot planet.

Violent volcanoes

There are enormous volcanoes on Venus. Some are much higher than any mountains on Earth. Venus's most famous volcano is called Maat Mons. It is more than five miles high. Sometimes all the volcanoes erupt at the same time, covering the whole planet in lava.

lava—rock that is so hot that it has melted

Lightning strikes

The air on Venus is full of deadly acid, and lightning flickers in the sky. Many spaceships have visited Venus, but they have been destroyed by the heat and acid in the air.

acid—*a substance that can eat away other substances*

Our planet, Earth

Earth is the planet that we live on. Most of its surface is covered with water, so from space Earth looks blue. Together, the water, air, and warmth from the Sun make life on Earth possible.

Life on Earth

There are more than 30 million different types of plants and animals on Earth. They live everywhere, from the deepest ocean to the top of the highest mountain.

dolphins

Restless planet

Compared to the other planets in the solar system, Earth has many volcanoes and earthquakes. Deep underground, Earth is so hot that the rock is molten. When a volcano erupts, the molten rock escapes onto the planet's surface.

molten—melted

Earth's Moon

The Moon is our closest neighbor in space. Just as Earth orbits the Sun, the Moon goes around planet Earth. There is no life or weather on the Moon—no clouds, wind, rain, or snow.

Hide-and-seek

The Moon takes one month to move around Earth. It also takes one month to spin around itself. Because of this, we only ever see one side of the Moon from Earth. However, spaceships have traveled around the Moon, so we know what the farside looks like.

weather—*how hot, cold, windy, dry, or rainy it is*

full Moon

gibbous Moon

last quarter

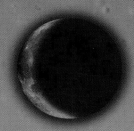
crescent Moon

Changing Moon

As the Moon moves, different parts of it are lit by the Sun. This makes it look like the Moon is changing shape. The different shapes are called phases.

Crusty craters

Most of the Moon's craters were made millions of years ago when huge chunks of rock crashed into it.

Moon visit

The Moon is the only other world people have visited. On the Moon astronauts weigh one sixth as much as they do on Earth.

Buzzing around
In 1969 Buzz Aldrin (born 1930) and Neil Armstrong (born 1930) were the first astronauts to land on the Moon. They stayed there for 21 hours before returning to Earth.

Lunar Rover

In 1971 an electric car called the *Lunar Rover* was used to explore the Moon. So far 12 people have visited the Moon. The last voyage was in 1972.

Famous footprints

Because there is no rain or wind to disturb the dust on the Moon's surface, the footprints left by the astronauts in 1969 are still there.

Rusty Mars

Mars is red because it is rusty. There is a lot of iron in the soil, and the air on Mars has made it turn red—just like rusty iron on Earth.

Poles of ice

Like Earth, the poles (the top and bottom ends of the planet) of Mars are covered in ice. The ice becomes thicker in the winter.

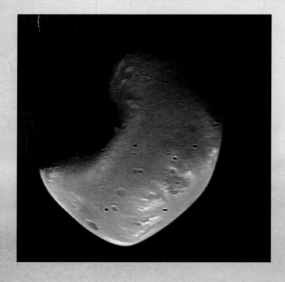

Two moons

Mars has two tiny moons called Phobos (left) and Deimos (above). Phobos is moving closer and closer to Mars, and scientists think that one day it will crash into Mars.

iron—a metal, often used for making things

Mighty Mons

The surface of Mars is covered with deserts, canyons, craters, and gigantic dead volcanoes. Olympus Mons is the tallest volcano in the solar system. It is 15 miles high.

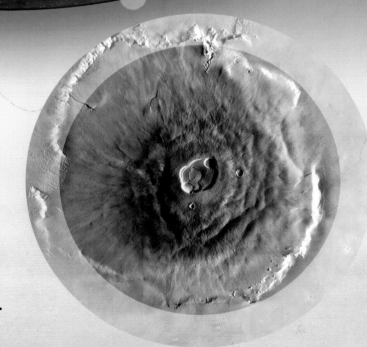

canyons—deep, rocky valleys

Living with **martians**

A long time ago the air on Mars was thicker, and there were valleys filled with water. This means that there may have been life on the red planet.

Super *Spirit*

In 2004 *Spirit* landed on Mars after a seven-month journey through space. It sent pictures of Mars back to Earth and studied the soil and rocks there.

space probes—*spaceships that explore space but do not carry astronauts*

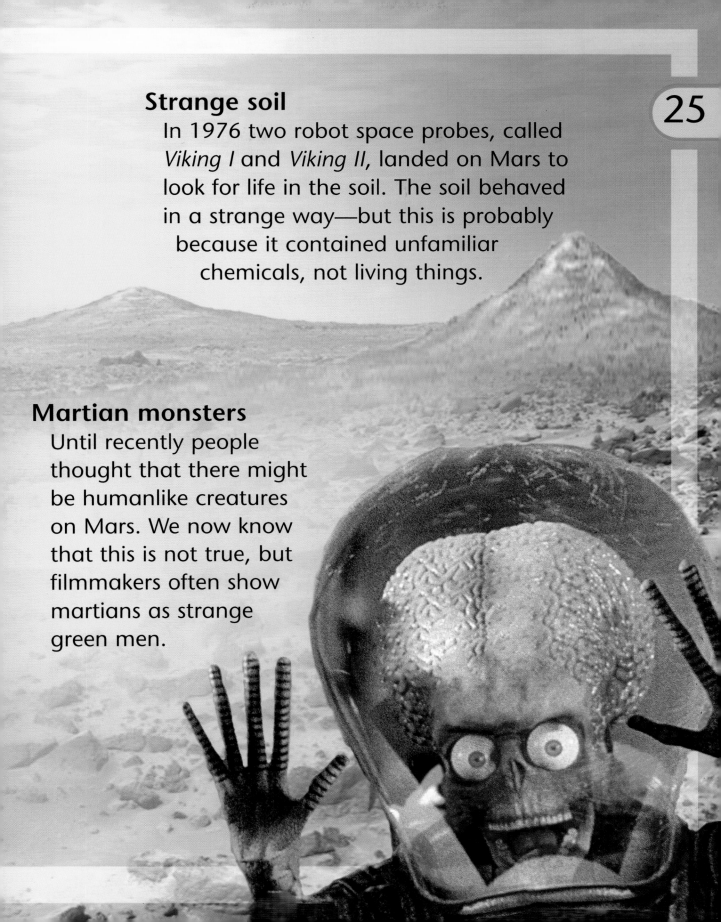

Strange soil

In 1976 two robot space probes, called *Viking I* and *Viking II*, landed on Mars to look for life in the soil. The soil behaved in a strange way—but this is probably because it contained unfamiliar chemicals, not living things.

Martian monsters

Until recently people thought that there might be humanlike creatures on Mars. We now know that this is not true, but filmmakers often show martians as strange green men.

Giant Jupiter

Jupiter is the biggest planet. It is 1,300 times the size of Earth. It spins around quickly, so its days are only ten hours long. Because it does not have a solid surface, it is impossible to land a spaceship on Jupiter.

Great Red Spot
Jupiter is a very stormy planet. One storm has already lasted for more than 300 years! From Earth, this storm looks like a giant red spot.

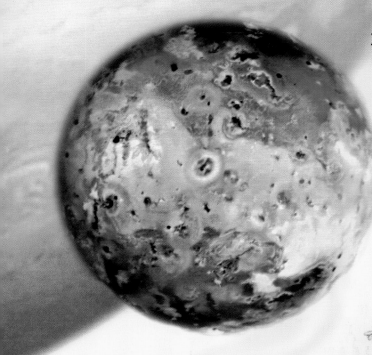

Marvelous moons

Jupiter has many moons. The moon shown here, Io, has active volcanoes. Europa has an icy surface, and Ganymede is the biggest moon in the solar system—it is even bigger than the planets Mercury and Pluto.

Great Galileo

In 1609, using a homemade telescope, Italian scientist Galileo Galilei (1564–1642) discovered four of Jupiter's moons.

telescope—an invention that makes things look bigger

Ringed Saturn

Many people think that Saturn is the most beautiful planet in the solar system. Saturn is so light that if there was an ocean big enough, the planet could float in it.

Rings of rock

Saturn's rings are made up of billions of pieces of rocks and dust. Although the planets Jupiter, Uranus, and Neptune also have ring systems, theirs are not as bright or as big as Saturn's.

billion—*one thousand million*

Studying Saturn

The *Cassini* space probe was launched in 1997 on a mission to study Saturn, its rings, and its moons. *Cassini* arrived in 2004.

Cold Uranus

Uranus is a huge, cold, blue-green world far out in space. It is surrounded by many black rings and icy moons. Because of the strange way it spins, nights on some parts of Uranus can last for more than 40 years.

Twisted Miranda

The surface of Miranda, one of Uranus's moons, is very uneven. It has cliffs that are more than 12 miles high and enormous ridges, grooves, and craters.

Uranus

groove—a long, thin line that is cut into a flat surface

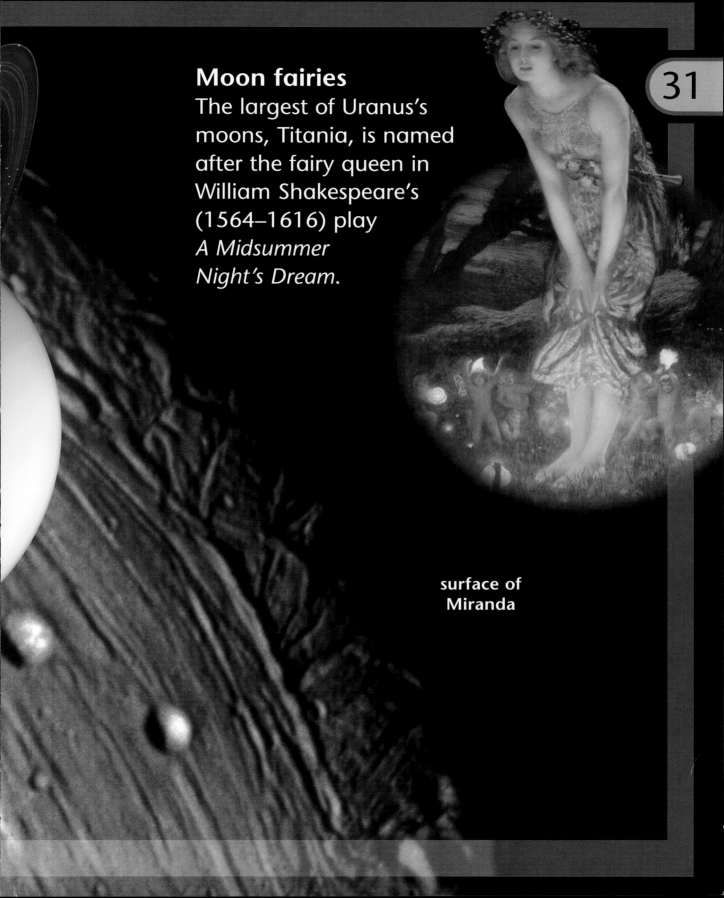

Moon fairies

The largest of Uranus's moons, Titania, is named after the fairy queen in William Shakespeare's (1564–1616) play *A Midsummer Night's Dream.*

surface of
Miranda

Stormy Neptune

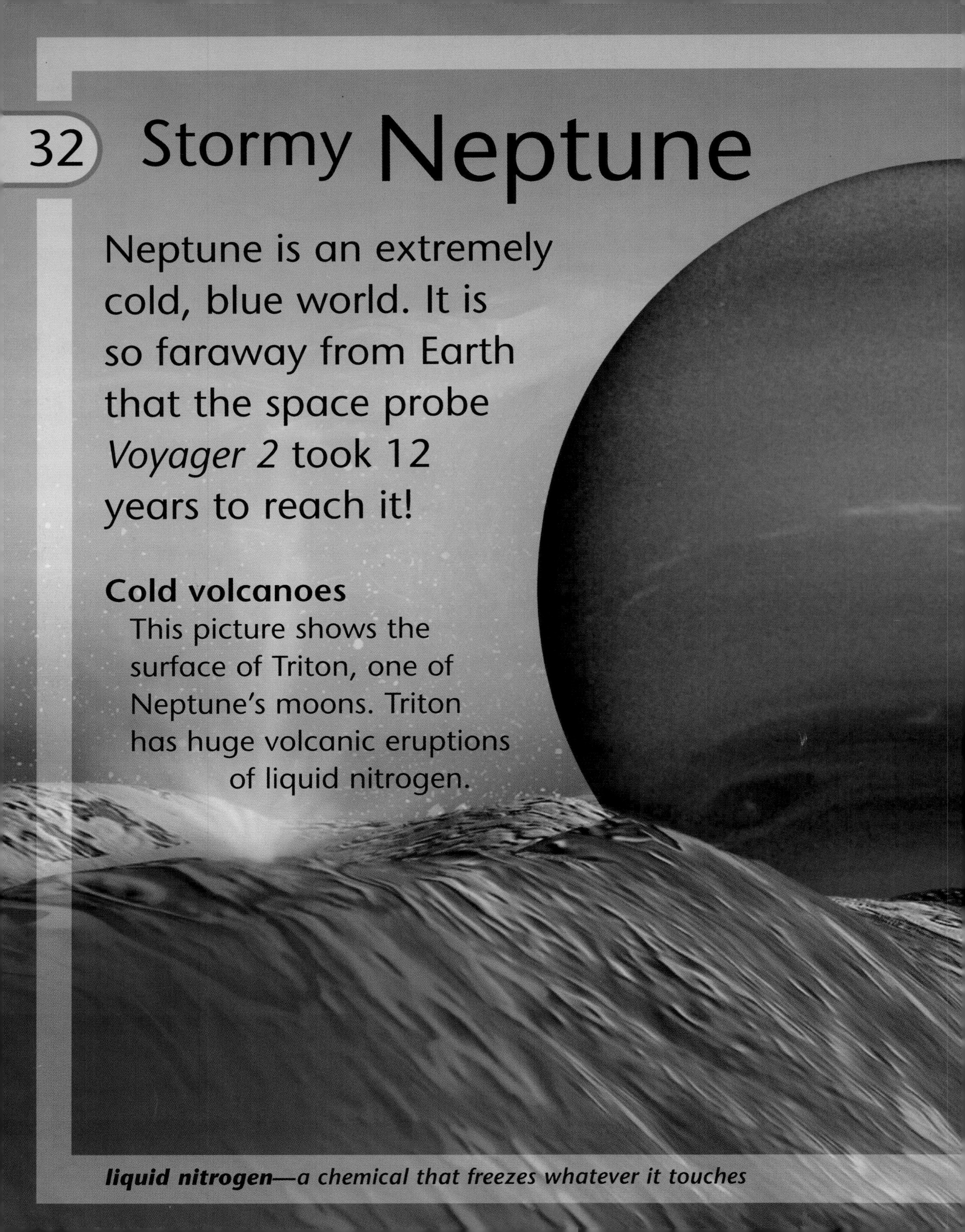

Neptune is an extremely cold, blue world. It is so faraway from Earth that the space probe *Voyager 2* took 12 years to reach it!

Cold volcanoes

This picture shows the surface of Triton, one of Neptune's moons. Triton has huge volcanic eruptions of liquid nitrogen.

liquid nitrogen—a chemical that freezes whatever it touches

Stormy clouds

Neptune is the stormiest
planet. The winds there
can blow up to 1,240 miles
per hour—three times as
fast as Earth's hurricanes!
Sometimes storm clouds
appear as white streaks
or dark spots on its
cloudy surface.

hurricane—a dangerous and violent storm with very high winds

Distant Pluto

Pluto is the planet farthest from the Sun. It is tiny, reddish-brown, and smaller than Earth's moon. Because it is so small and distant, Pluto can only be seen from Earth by using a powerful telescope.

Colossal Charon

Pluto has an enormous moon called Charon. This giant was only discovered in 1978. Charon is darker and grayer than Pluto, but like Pluto, it is also covered in rocks and ice.

In the dark

If you visited Pluto, the Sun would look like a bright star. Pluto is so faraway from the Sun that it is always dark. It is the only planet that no spaceship has reached, so we do not know what it really looks like.

Failed planet

Beyond Mars and Jupiter there are billions of pieces of rock and metal called asteroids. They are much smaller than planets. Scientists believe that the asteroids are pieces of a planet that failed to form.

Asteroid belt

Most asteroids can be found in two regions, or "belts." One of the belts is between Mars and Jupiter, and the other is beyond Neptune.

region—area

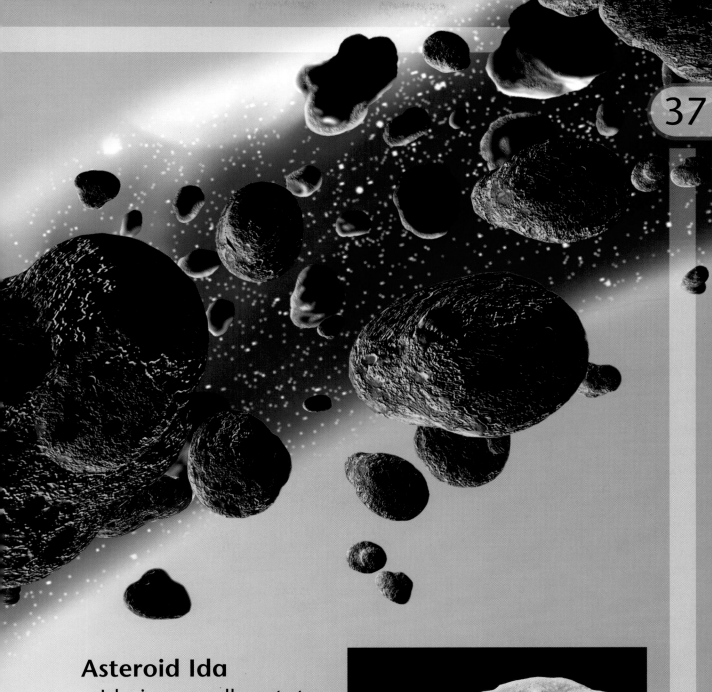

Asteroid Ida

Ida is a small, potato-shaped asteroid with its own tiny moon. In 1993 the *Galileo* space probe took pictures of Ida as it flew past.

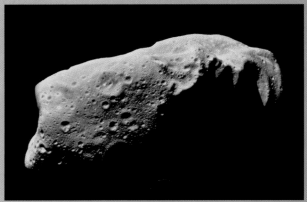

Space
travelers

Comets are visitors from the outer parts of the solar system. They are lumps of ice and dust—a little like dirty icebergs drifting through space. When the comets are close to the Sun, the ice turns into gas.

Return of the comet

All comets orbit the Sun. Some take hundreds, thousands, or even millions of years to return. Halley's Comet only returns every 76 years. This famous tapestry shows Halley's Comet (top left) in 1066.

Two-tailed Hale-Bopp

As a comet moves closer to the Sun, it forms two tails. One of the tails is made up of gas and the other of dust. The gas tail points away from the Sun. In this picture of Comet Hale-Bopp the gas tail is blue, and the dust tail is whitish.

Comet crash!

In 1994 pieces of a comet called Shoemaker-Levy 9 broke apart and crashed into Jupiter. This left patches in Jupiter's atmosphere that lasted for many months.

Space rubble

There are many pieces of rock and dust drifting in space. These objects are called meteoroids. Many meteoroids are left behind by comets.

Shooting stars!

Every year 200,000 tons of meteoroids fall through Earth's atmosphere. As large meteoroids rush through the air, they become so hot that they glow. This falling glow is called a meteor or a shooting star.

ton—2,210 pounds

Huge Hoba

Meteors that land on Earth are called meteorites. The heaviest known meteorite is Hoba West. It was found in 1920 in Namibia, Africa, and weighs around 60 tons—that is as heavy as nine elephants!

Way out there

In 1961 a Russian named Yuri Gagarin (1934–1968) became the first person to journey into space and travel right around Earth. Since then many astronauts have traveled through space.

Drifting through space

Exploring space is dangerous. Sometimes astronauts leave their spaceships to "walk" in space. This astronaut is wearing a device that can push him back to his spaceship if he starts to drift away.

Life in space

In space there is no air, nothing has any weight, and there is no "up" or "down," which can make life difficult. Some space travelers get "space sick," just like people on Earth get seasick.

Shining **stars**

Bedroom planetarium

Dome-shaped buildings called planetariums have lights that show the night sky. Use a flashlight to make your own starry sky.

You will need
- Flashlight
- Pencil
- Black poster board and piece of white paper
- Scissors
- Tape

Place the flashlight on the poster board so that you can trace around the front side of it. Using a pencil, carefully trace around the flashlight.

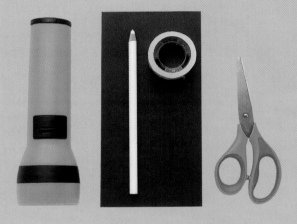

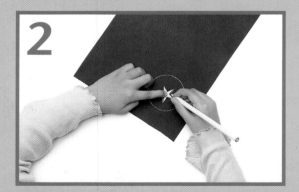

To make a star-shaped stencil, draw a star on a piece of white paper and cut it out. Place the stencil inside the flashlight shape and draw around it.

Using the scissors, carefully cut out both shapes. You should now be left with poster board that has a star shape in the middle.

Use tape to attach the poster board to the front of the flashlight. Turn off all the lights and shine the flashlight on the ceiling to create a beautiful starry sky. For something different try cutting out a shape of the Moon.

Watch the Moon

Find the craters!
Not only are there craters on the surface of the Moon, but every month our closest neighbor also changes shape. On a clear night use binoculars to look for the Moon's craters. Never look at the Sun with binoculars because this could damage your eyes.

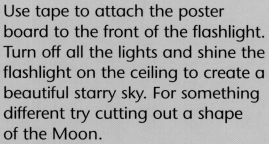

Whenever you see the Moon—whether at night or during the day—draw its shape on the correct date in a calendar. After a few months your calendar will show you how the Moon goes through a series of changes (called phases).

Crazy comets

Finding new comets
New comets are discovered
every year, but most of them
are too faint to see without
using binoculars or a telescope.

1

To make big pieces of space dust,
place two sugar cookies on a plate.
Using the wooden spoon, crush the
cookies into large pieces.

You will need
- 2 large plates
- Sugar cookies
- Wooden spoon
- Teaspoon
- Colored sprinkles
- Chocolate sprinkles
- Ice-cream scoop
- Chocolate ice cream
- Ice-cream cone

2

To make smaller pieces of
space dust, add a large handful
of colored sprinkles to the
crushed cookies.

3

For extra space dust add two
handfuls of chocolate sprinkles
to the mixture. Mix the space
dust using a teaspoon.

4

For the comet's head use an ice-cream scoop to make a ball of ice cream. Cover the head in the space dust mixture.

6

To make the comet's tail, carefully place the ice-cream ball onto an ice-cream cone. Push down lightly on top of the ball to secure it.

5

Roll the ice cream back into a ball shape. If the ice cream has started to melt, put it on another plate in the freezer.

Although you would never be able to eat a real comet, such as Hale-Bopp, this one is made from delicious ice cream, so it tastes great!

Index